Mastering Your Finances

A Comprehensive Guide to Financial Stability

By

Zakari Umar

"Mastering Your Finances: A Comprehensive Guide to Financial Stability" is a valuable resource for individuals seeking to improve their financial well-being. The book covers essential topics such as assessing one's financial situation, creating a budget, reducing debt, building savings, increasing income, and managing credit effectively. With its practical approach and actionable advice, the author provides readers with the necessary tools to take control of their finances and achieve long-term financial stability. Whether you are just starting your financial journey or seeking to enhance your current strategies, this book offers valuable insights that can benefit individuals of all financial backgrounds.

Contents

INTRODUCTION

Chapter One

Chapter Two

Chapter Three

Chapter Four

Chapter Five

Chapter Six

Chapter Seven

INTRODUCTION

Importance of Financial Stability

Have you ever felt like you barely kept your head above water regarding your finances? Maybe you're constantly worrying about how you will pay the bills or save for the future. Or perhaps you're carrying a heavy debt that seems to keep growing. Whatever your financial situation, I'm here to tell you that financial stability is important – and achievable!

So, what is financial stability, exactly? At its core, financial stability is about having control over your finances and maintaining a balance between your income and expenses. It means having a financial cushion to weather unexpected expenses and planning for the future without worrying about the present. Achieving financial stability takes effort and planning, but it's well worth it. Here's why:

First and foremost, financial stability provides us with a sense of security. When we have a handle on our finances, we can better deal with life's ups and downs. Whether it's an unexpected car repair or a sudden job loss, having a financial cushion can help us weather the storm without adding stress or worry. On the other hand, if we're living paycheck to paycheck and have no savings to fall back on, any unexpected expense can send us into a spiral of debt and anxiety. By achieving financial stability, we can reduce the impact of financial stress on our lives and feel more secure in our ability to handle whatever life throws our way.

Financial stability also gives us a sense of control over our lives. When we control our finances, we can better make informed decisions about spending, saving, and investing. This, in turn, can help us achieve our goals and pursue our dreams. Whether buying a home, starting a business, or saving for retirement, having a solid financial foundation can make all the difference. Without financial stability, we may feel like we're constantly struggling to keep up with bills and expenses and unable to pursue our dreams.

In addition to providing security and control, financial stability is also essential for our mental health and well-being. Financial stress is a major source of anxiety and depression, affecting physical and mental health. When we're constantly worried about money, it cannot be easy to focus on anything else. Research has shown that financial stress can lead to higher rates of absenteeism, decreased productivity, and lower job satisfaction. By achieving financial stability, we can reduce the impact of financial stress on our lives, leading to better overall health and well-being.

Another benefit of financial stability is long-term wealth building. By managing our finances effectively, we can grow our wealth through investments, savings, and smart spending decisions. This, in turn, can provide financial freedom and flexibility, allowing us to pursue our passions, travel, and enjoy retirement without financial worry. By contrast, a lack of financial stability can lead to a cycle of debt and missed opportunities, making it difficult to build wealth over time.

Common financial challenges people face

Let's talk about some common financial challenges that people face. Money can be a tricky subject, and it's not uncommon to run into roadblocks along the way. Here are a few challenges that you might be facing:

1. Debt: One of the biggest financial challenges people face is managing debt. Whether it's credit card debt, student loans, or a mortgage, owing money can feel overwhelming. Finding a strategy to pay off your debt can be a long and

difficult process, but it's worth it to regain financial stability.

2. Living paycheck to paycheck: Many people struggle to make ends meet and live paycheck to paycheck. This can make it difficult to save money, plan for the future, and deal with unexpected expenses.

3. Lack of financial literacy: Not everyone knows to make smart financial decisions. This can lead to overspending, insufficient savings, or investing in the wrong places.

4. Unemployment or underemployment: Losing a job or not being able to find work that pays enough can be a huge financial challenge. It can be difficult to make ends meet without a steady source of income.

5. Medical expenses: Healthcare costs can be a huge financial burden, especially if you have a chronic illness or need expensive treatments. Even with insurance, medical bills can quickly add up and cause financial stress.

These are just a few examples of the financial challenges that many people face. The important thing is to recognize that you're not alone in your struggles, and in this book, you have the resources and strategies to help you overcome these challenges. Whether seeking financial advice, finding ways to increase your income, or creating a budget to manage your expenses, you will have all the steps to improve your financial situation.

Overview of the book's approach and contents

This book is a comprehensive guide to personal finance management that covers everything from assessing your current financial situation to managing your credit card. The approach of the book is to provide readers with practical advice and strategies that they can apply in their daily lives to achieve financial stability.

In the first chapter of this book, we dive into a crucial aspect of financial planning: understanding your income, expenses, debt, and savings. By analyzing these factors, you can better understand your financial situation and identify areas for improvement. This is an essential first step toward creating a solid financial plan. Without a clear understanding of your income and expenses, it's impossible to make informed financial decisions. By analyzing your finances, you can identify areas where you might overspend or underutilize your resources.

This knowledge can then be used to make adjustments and optimize your budget. Another critical aspect of financial planning is managing your debt and savings. By understanding your debt load and creating a plan to pay it off, you can reduce your financial stress and improve your overall financial health. Similarly, by identifying your savings goals and creating a plan to achieve them, you can work towards a more secure financial future.

If you want to take control of your finances and achieve your financial goals, Chapter 2 is worth checking out! The chapter dives into the importance of creating a budget and how it can be a game-changer when managing your money. This chapter covers various topics, from setting financial goals to creating a monthly budget that works for you. It's helpful if you're starting with budgeting or looking to improve your skills.

Next in this book, you will see some useful strategies for reducing debt, including consolidation options and avoiding future debt

In Chapter 4 of our financial guide, we will dive into the importance of building your savings. It's crucial if you want to achieve your long-term financial goals.

The next chapter, chapter 5, is about helping you increase your income, which most of us could help with.

In Chapter 6, we'll be talking all about managing credit. This includes understanding your credit score and report, building and improving your credit, and using credit responsibly.

Finally, we'll wrap up the book by reviewing key takeaways. We want to ensure you feel equipped to continue working towards your financial goals after finishing the book.

Chapter One

Assessing Your Current Financial Situation

Understanding your income and expenses

Managing your finances can be a daunting task, but taking the time to understand your income and expenses is the first step to gaining control over your financial future.

Let's start by talking about income. Income is any money you earn from working, investing, or any other source. Your income is an important factor in determining your financial health and can affect your ability to pay bills, save for the future, and make important purchases. Understanding your income is important to make informed decisions about managing it.

To start understanding your income, you should first determine your gross income. This is the money you earn before taxes and deductions are taken out. For most people, their gross income is their salary or hourly wage. However, if you have any additional sources of income, such as rental or investment, you should include those in your gross income as well.

Once you have determined your gross income, you can calculate your net income. This is the amount left over after taxes and deductions are taken out. Your net income is the money you take home each pay period.

Understanding your income is important, but it's equally important to understand your expenses. Expenses are any costs you incur, including bills, groceries, rent, and other everyday expenses. Understanding your expenses is essential to managing your finances and ensuring you have enough money to cover your bills and save for the future.

To start understanding your expenses, you should first list all your monthly expenses. This should include everything from your rent or mortgage payment to your cell phone bill, groceries, and any other regular expenses you have. Once you have a list of your monthly expenses, you can then calculate your total monthly expenses.

It's important to remember that your expenses can vary from month to month, so it's a good idea to track your expenses over time. This will give you a better understanding of your spending habits and help you identify areas where you can cut back if necessary.

Once you have a good understanding of your income and expenses, you can then start creating a budget. A budget is a plan that helps you allocate your income toward your expenses and savings goals. A budget can help you stay on track and avoid overspending.

To create a budget, start by listing all your income sources and your monthly expenses. Then, allocate your income toward your expenses, starting with your most important bills, such as rent or mortgage payments. Once you have allocated your income toward your expenses, you can determine how much money you have left over for savings and other discretionary spending.

It's important to be realistic when creating your budget. Don't try to allocate more money toward your expenses than you can realistically afford. If your expenses exceed your income, you may need to make some adjustments, such as cutting back on discretionary spending or finding ways to increase your income.

Once you have created a budget, it's important to stick to it. This means keeping track of your spending and making adjustments as necessary. If you overspend in a particular category, you may need to cut back on that area or find ways to save money.

In addition to creating a budget, there are other steps you can take to manage your income and expenses. For example, you can set up automatic payments for your bills to ensure they are paid on time each month. You can also set up a savings account to automatically transfer money from your checking account each month.

Another important step in managing your finances is to build an emergency fund. An emergency fund is a savings account that you can use to cover unexpected expenses, such as car repairs or medical bills. Ideally, it would be best to aim to have at least three to six months' worth of living expenses saved in your emergency fund. This will help you avoid debt or having to dip into your other savings to cover unexpected expenses.

In addition to building an emergency fund, it's important to prioritize saving for the future. This might include saving for retirement, a down payment on a house, or your children's education. By setting specific savings goals and contributing to them regularly, you can ensure that you are on track to meet your financial goals.

It's important to regularly review your income and expenses to ensure that you are staying on track. This might involve revisiting your budget every few months to make adjustments or reviewing your savings and investment accounts to ensure that you are on track to meet your goals.

Analyzing your debt and savings

Managing your finances can be overwhelming, but understanding your debt and savings is a critical step toward financial stability and independence.

Let's start by discussing debt. Debt is any money you owe someone else, such as a credit card balance, student loan, or mortgage. While debt can sometimes be a necessary part of achieving certain goals, such as buying a home or pursuing higher education, it can also be a significant financial burden if not managed properly.

To analyze your debt, you should list all your outstanding debts, including the creditor, interest rate, and minimum payment due. Once you have a clear understanding of your debts, you can then prioritize them based on their interest rates and payment terms.

It's important to remember that not all debt is created equal. Some types of debt, such as credit card debt, can carry high-interest rates and fees, making them more expensive over time. Other types of debt, such as student loans or mortgages, may have lower interest rates but can still significantly impact your finances over time.

To manage your debt effectively, it's important to prioritize paying off high-interest debt first. This might involve making larger payments on your credit card balance or consolidating high-interest debt into a lower-interest loan. By reducing your high-interest debt, you can save money on interest over time and free up more money for savings and other expenses.

Once you plan to pay off your debt, it's important to stick to it. This might involve making a budget and cutting back on discretionary spending to free up more money for debt repayment. It may also involve increasing your income, such as working part-time or selling unwanted items.

In addition to managing your debt, prioritizing savings is important. Savings can provide a financial cushion in case of unexpected expenses or emergencies and help you achieve your long-term financial goals.

To analyze your savings, you should first list all your savings accounts, including your checking, emergency fund, and investment accounts. Once you have a clear understanding of your savings, you can then prioritize your savings goals based on your short-term and long-term needs.

Short-term savings might include an emergency fund or a down payment on a large purchase, such as a car or home. Long-term savings might include retirement savings or college savings for your children.

To build your savings, it's important to set specific savings goals and contribute to them regularly. This might involve setting up automatic transfers from your checking account to your savings accounts or setting aside a portion of each paycheck for savings.

In addition to saving regularly, it's also important to maximize your savings by choosing the right savings and investment accounts. This might involve choosing a high-yield savings account or investing in a diversified portfolio of stocks and bonds.

Managing your debt and savings can be a complex process, but tools and resources are available to help you along the way. For example, some online tools and apps can help you track your spending, create a budget, and monitor your savings and investments.

It's also important to seek professional advice if you're unsure about how to manage your debt and savings effectively. A financial advisor can help you create a personalized plan based on your financial goals and circumstances.

Identifying areas for improvement

Identifying areas for improvement is a critical step toward achieving your financial goals. Whether you want to save for a down payment on a home, pay off debt, or build an emergency fund, identifying areas for improvement can help you create a plan to get there.

So, how can you identify areas for improvement in your finances? Here are a few tips to get started:

1. Track your spending: One of the best ways to identify areas for improvement is to track your spending. This can help you understand where your money is going and where you might be overspending. You can use a budgeting app, a spreadsheet, or even pen and paper to track your spending for a few weeks or months. Once you clearly understand your spending habits, you can start identifying areas where you can cut back. For example, if you notice you're spending a lot on eating out, you might aim to cook at home more often to save money.

2. Review your bills: Another way to identify areas for improvement is to review your bills and expenses. Are

there any bills you're paying for services you're not using or don't need? For example, are you paying for a gym membership you haven't used in months? Reviewing your bills can help you identify areas where you might be able to cut back and save money. This might involve negotiating with your service providers or canceling services that you're not using.

3. Evaluate your debt: Debt can be a significant financial burden, so it's important to evaluate your debt to identify areas for improvement. This might involve reviewing your interest rates and payment terms to determine if there are opportunities to refinance or consolidate your debt. It might also involve creating a plan to pay off high-interest debt first, such as credit card debt. By prioritizing your debt repayment, you can save on interest and free up more money for savings and other expenses.

4. Assess your savings: Savings are an important part of financial stability, so it's important to assess your savings to identify areas for improvement. This might involve evaluating your emergency fund to determine if you

have enough saved to cover unexpected expenses. It might also involve setting specific savings goals, such as saving for a down payment on a home or for retirement. By setting specific savings goals and contributing to them regularly, you can ensure you're on track to achieve your financial goals.

5. Seek professional advice: If you're unsure about how to identify areas for improvement or create a plan to achieve your financial goals, it's important to seek professional advice. A financial advisor can help you evaluate your finances and create a personalized plan based on your specific goals and circumstances.

Chapter Two

Creating a Budget

Setting financial goals

It's an essential step towards achieving financial success and creating a stable future for yourself. Financial goals are an important aspect of financial planning. Setting them can help you focus your efforts on what you want to achieve financially and create a roadmap for achieving those goals. Here's what you need to know about setting financial goals.

Identify your financial priorities

The first step in setting financial goals is identifying what's important to you. This could include paying off debt, saving for retirement, buying a house, or starting a business. Once you've identified your priorities, you can start to set specific, measurable goals that will help you achieve them.

Set SMART goals

When setting financial goals, it's important to use the SMART framework. SMART stands for Specific, Measurable, Achievable, Relevant, and Time-bound. Here's what each of these elements means:

- Specific: Your goal should be clear and specific. Instead of setting a vague goal like "save money," be specific about what you want to save for, such as "save $10,000 for a down payment on a house."

- Measurable: Your goal should be quantifiable so that you can track your progress. For example, "save $500 per month for the next 12 months" is a measurable goal.

- Achievable: Your goal should be achievable based on your current financial situation. If you're in debt, it might not be realistic to save $10,000 in a year. Instead, you might set a goal to pay off a certain amount of debt each month.

- Relevant: Your goal should be relevant to your overall financial plan. For example, if your goal is to retire in 20 years, saving for a down payment on a house might not be as relevant as saving for retirement.

- Time-bound: Your goal should have a specific deadline so that you have a target to work towards. For example, "save $10,000 for a down payment on a house within the next two years" is time-bound.

Prioritize your goals

Once you've set your financial goals, prioritize them based on their importance and urgency. For example, if you have high-interest credit card debt, paying it off should be a top priority before you start saving for other goals.

Create a plan

Now that you've identified your financial priorities and set SMART goals, it's time to create a plan for achieving them. This might involve creating a budget, increasing your income, or reducing expenses. The key is to be realistic and create a plan to stick to.

Monitor your progress

It's important to monitor your progress toward your financial goals regularly. This will help you stay on track and make adjustments if necessary. For example, if you're not on track to meet your savings goal, you might need to adjust your budget or find ways to increase your income.

Celebrate your achievements

Finally, celebrate your achievements along the way. Setting and achieving financial goals can be a challenging process, so it's important to take the time to recognize your progress and celebrate your successes.

Creating a monthly budget

Creating a monthly budget can seem like a daunting task, but it's a really important step in taking control of your finances. It can help you track your expenses, manage your money, and save for future goals.

To start, you'll want to gather all your financial information. This includes your income, bills, debts, and other expenses. Take some time to go through your bank statements and receipts to make sure you have a clear understanding of where your money is going each month.

Once you have all your information, it's time to start budgeting. Begin by calculating your monthly income and subtracting your fixed expenses, such as rent, utilities, and any other bills you have to pay each month. This will show you how much money you have left to work with.

Next, take a look at your variable expenses. These are things like groceries, transportation, entertainment, and other expenses that fluctuate from month to month. Decide on a reasonable amount you can allocate towards each category, and stick to it throughout the month.

It's also important to plan for unexpected expenses. Set aside some money in a separate savings account or category in your budget for emergencies, such as car repairs or medical bills.

- *Track expenses*: As you start implementing your budget, track your expenses and adjust your budget as needed. You may need to allocate more money to certain categories or cut back on others.

  Remember, creating a monthly budget is all about being intentional with your money and setting yourself up for financial success. By taking control of your finances and planning, you'll be able to reach your goals and enjoy peace of mind knowing you're on the right track.

- *Prioritize:* Another helpful tip when creating a monthly budget is prioritizing your expenses. Make sure to cover the necessities, such as rent, utilities, and food. Then, you can allocate money towards discretionary spending, such as entertainment or shopping.

- *Long-term goals:* It's also important to consider your long-term financial goals when creating a budget. If you have a goal of saving for a down payment on a house or paying off debt, make sure to include those expenses in your budget and allocate money towards them each month.

- *Be realistic:* When creating a budget, it's important to be realistic about your expenses and income. Don't underestimate your expenses or overestimate your income, as this can lead to a budget that's impossible to stick to.

- *Automate Savings:* Another helpful tip is to automate your savings and bill payments. Set up automatic payments for your bills and automate your savings so that a certain amount is automatically transferred to your savings account each month.

- *Review regularly:* don't forget to review your budget regularly. It's important to see how well you're sticking to your budget and make adjustments as needed. If you're consistently overspending in a certain category, consider adjusting your budget or finding ways to reduce expenses.

Tracking your expenses and adjusting your budget

Tracking your expenses is an important habit to develop to stay on top of your finances. By tracking how much you're spending and where your money is going, you can identify areas where you may be overspending and make adjustments accordingly.

There are a few different methods you can use to track your expenses. One popular option is to use a budgeting app or tool, such as Mint or YNAB. These apps allow you to connect your bank accounts and credit cards so that your transactions are automatically categorized and tracked. You can also set up alerts for when you're getting close to reaching your budget limits in different categories.

If you prefer a more manual approach, you can also track your expenses using a spreadsheet or pen and paper. Write down your expenses as you make them, and categorize them into different categories such as housing, transportation, food, and entertainment.

Once you've been tracking your expenses for a few weeks or months, you can analyze your spending patterns and look for areas where you can cut back. For example, you may notice that you're spending a lot on eating out or subscription services and decide to reduce those expenses to save money.

Adjusting your budget can be a bit of a balancing act. On the one hand, you want to be realistic about what you can afford and set a budget to stick to. On the other hand, you also want to make sure that your budget is helping you to achieve your financial goals, whether that's paying off debt, saving for a down payment on a house, or building up an emergency fund.

One approach that can be helpful is to start with a baseline budget that covers all of your necessary expenses, such as housing, utilities, and food. Then, consider your discretionary expenses and decide which ones are most important. You may need to make some trade-offs to stay within your budget, but the key is to find a balance that works for you.

Chapter Three
Reducing Debt

Strategies for paying off debt

Paying off debt can be a daunting task, but with the right strategies in place, it's doable.

First and foremost, it's important to make a budget. You need to know exactly how much money you have coming in and how much goes out each month. From there, you can determine how much money you have to put toward your debt. This may require adjusting your spending habits, but the end goal of becoming debt-free will be worth it in the long run.

Once you have a budget, it's time to prioritize your debts. List out all of your debts, including the balances and interest rates. From there, you can decide which debts to pay off first. One popular method is the debt snowball method, where you focus on paying off the smallest debt first, then moving on to the next smallest, and so on. Another option is the debt avalanche method, where you focus on paying off the debt with the highest interest rate first, then moving on to the next highest, and so on. Both methods can be effective, so choose the one that makes the most sense.

It's also important to consider consolidating your debts. Consolidating your debts can simplify the repayment process by combining all of your debts into one monthly payment, often with a lower interest rate. This can help you save money on interest and make it easier to keep track of your payments.

Another strategy to consider is increasing your income. This can be done by taking on a side hustle, asking for a raise at work, or even selling some of your belongings you no longer need. Any extra money you can put towards your debts will help you pay them off faster.

Finally, it's important to stay motivated and track your progress. Celebrate your small victories along the way, and don't get discouraged if it takes longer than you initially thought. Paying off debt is a journey, but with the right strategies and mindset, you can get there!

Consolidation options

Consolidating your debts can be a great option if you're looking to simplify your repayment process and potentially save money on interest. There are a few different consolidation options to consider, so let's take a look!

One option is a balance transfer credit card. This involves transferring the balances of your high-interest credit cards to a new card with a lower interest rate. This can help you save money on interest and make it easier to keep track of your payments, as you'll only have one monthly payment to worry about. However, it's important to read the fine print and make sure you understand any fees associated with the balance transfer, as well as the new card's interest rate, once the introductory period ends.

Another option is a personal loan. This involves taking out a loan to pay off your debts, then making one monthly payment towards the new loan. Personal loans can have lower interest rates than credit cards, which can help you save on interest over time. However, it's important to ensure the loan has a lower interest rate than your existing debts. Otherwise, you may end up paying more in interest over time.

If you own a home, you may also consider a home equity loan or line of credit. This involves using the equity in your home to take out a loan to pay off your debts. Home equity loans and lines of credit can have lower interest rates than other loans, but they also come with the risk of losing your home if you can't make your payments.

It's important to do your research and consider all of your options before deciding on a consolidation option. Make sure you understand the fees, interest rates, and terms of any new loans or credit cards you're considering, and make sure you're comfortable with the repayment plan. With the right consolidation option, you can simplify your repayment process and work towards becoming debt-free!

Avoiding future debt

Debt is a common problem many people face, and it cannot be easy to overcome once you're in it. However, there are steps you can take to avoid getting into debt in the first place. By being proactive and making smart financial decisions, you can set yourself up for long-term financial stability and avoid the stress and burden that comes with being in debt.

- One of the most important things you can do to avoid future debt is to create and stick to a budget. This means tracking your income and expenses and ensuring your spending doesn't exceed your income. By clearly understanding your finances, you can identify areas where you can cut back on expenses and save money.

- When creating your budget, it's important to prioritize your spending. Ensure you cover your essential expenses, such as rent or mortgage payments, utilities, and food. Then, you can allocate money for discretionary spending, such as entertainment or hobbies.

- Another key to avoiding debt is to build up an emergency fund. This is money that you set aside specifically for unexpected expenses, such as car repairs or medical bills. With an emergency fund, you can avoid relying on credit cards or other forms of debt when unexpected expenses arise.

In addition to creating a budget and building an emergency fund, there are other steps you can take to avoid future debt. Here are a few tips:

1. Avoid impulse purchases: It can be tempting to make impulse purchases, but these can quickly add up and lead to debt. Before making a purchase, ask yourself if it's something you really need or if it's just a want.

2. Use credit cards wisely: Credit cards can be a useful tool for building credit, but they can also be a source of debt if not used wisely. Make sure to pay your balance in full each month and avoid carrying a balance on your card.

3. Save for big purchases: If you plan to make a big purchase, such as a new car or home, save for it well in advance. This can help you avoid taking on debt to make the purchase.

4. Live within your means: It's important to live within your means and not try to keep up with others who may have more money or a different lifestyle. By focusing on what you can afford and what's important to you, you can avoid overspending and going into debt.

5. Seek professional advice: If you're struggling with debt or want to learn more about managing your finances, consider seeking advice from a financial professional. They can provide guidance and resources to help you make smart financial decisions.

Chapter Four

Building Your Savings

Setting up an emergency fund

Setting up an emergency fund is a great step toward improving your financial situation. It's a wise financial decision that can help you deal with unexpected expenses and tough times without relying on credit cards or loans. In setting up an emergency fund;

1. Determine your emergency fund goal: First, decide how much money you want to save for your emergency fund. A good rule of thumb is to aim for 3-6 months' living expenses. You can calculate this by adding up all of your monthly bills, including rent or mortgage payments, utilities, food, transportation, and any other necessary expenses. Then, multiply that amount by the months you want to save.

2. Choose the right type of account: Next, you need to choose the right type of account to save your emergency fund. You want an account that is easily accessible but not too easily accessible that you will be tempted to dip into it for non-emergency expenses. High-yield

savings or a money market account are good options because they offer higher interest rates than traditional savings accounts and allow you to withdraw your money quickly if needed.

3. Start saving regularly: Now that you have a goal and a savings account, it's time to start saving regularly. You can automatically transfer your checking account to your emergency fund account weekly or monthly. This way, you won't have to think about saving money; it will happen automatically.

4. Keep adding to your emergency fund: As you work on building your emergency fund, keep adding to it whenever you can. This can include windfalls such as bonuses, tax refunds, or gifts. The more you can save, the better prepared you will be for unexpected expenses.

5. Use your emergency fund wisely: Finally, if an emergency does arise, make sure you use your emergency fund wisely. Only use it for emergencies, such as unexpected medical bills, car repairs, or job loss. Avoid using it for non-essential expenses, such as vacations or luxury purchases.

Saving for long-term goals

If you have long-term goals that you want to achieve, such as buying a home, saving for retirement, or starting a business, it's important to start saving early and regularly. Here are some tips on how to save for your long-term goals:

1. Define your goals: First, you need to define your long-term goals and estimate how much money you will need to achieve them. This will help you set a savings target and determine how much you need to save each month.

2. Create a budget: Next, create a budget that considers your income, expenses, and savings goals. Be sure to prioritize your long-term goals and allocate a portion of your income towards saving for them.

3. Start early: The earlier you save, the more time your money has to grow. Even if you can only afford to save a small amount each month, it's better than not saving at all.

4. Please choose the right savings account: When saving for long-term goals, it's important to choose the right one. Look for accounts that offer high-interest

rates, low fees, and flexibility to access your money when you need it.

5. Automate your savings: One of the easiest ways to save for long-term goals is to automate your savings. Set up automatic transfers from your checking account to your savings account regularly. This way, you won't have to think about saving money; it will happen automatically.

6. Increase your savings over time: As your income grows or your expenses decrease, try to increase your monthly savings. This will help you reach your savings goals faster.

7. Stay focused: Saving for long-term goals can be long and sometimes challenging. Stay focused on your goals and remind yourself why you're saving. This will help you stay motivated and on track.

Remember, saving for long-term goals requires discipline and patience.

Investing in the future

Investing is an important way to build wealth and prepare for your financial future. Whether you're looking to save for retirement, purchase a home, or build a nest egg, investing can help you achieve those goals.

One of the first things to consider when investing is your risk tolerance. This refers to how comfortable you are with the ups and downs of the stock market. Generally, the higher the potential returns, the higher the risk. So, if you're willing to take on more risk, you may want to consider investing in stocks that can offer higher returns but also come with more volatility. On the other hand, if you're more risk-averse, you may prefer to invest in bonds, which offer lower returns but are generally considered safer.

Another important aspect of investing is diversification. This means spreading your money across different types of investments, such as stocks, bonds, real estate, and commodities. By diversifying, you can help reduce your overall risk and potentially increase your returns.

It's also important to consider the fees associated with investing. Some investment products, such as mutual funds and exchange-traded funds (ETFs), charge fees that can eat into your returns over time. Read the fine print and understand the fees associated with any investment products you're considering.

Finally, it's important to have a long-term perspective on investing. While it can be tempting to try to time the market or make quick gains, investing is a marathon, not a sprint. By staying invested for the long term and resisting the urge to make impulsive decisions based on short-term market fluctuations, you can help ensure that your investments have time to grow and compound over time.

Chapter Five

Increasing Your Income

In today's fast-paced and expensive world, meeting financial obligations can often feel daunting. Budgeting is certainly an essential practice that helps individuals stay within their means and manage their expenses effectively. However, it's equally important to explore opportunities for increasing income to create a more stable and prosperous financial future.

While sticking to a budget can help control spending and ensure that bills are paid on time, it often leaves little room for savings or investments. By actively seeking ways to boost your income, you open up new possibilities to not only cover unforeseen expenses but also create a solid foundation for long-term financial growth.

There are several methods to boost your earnings, including:

Negotiating a salary raise

Negotiating a salary raise might seem intimidating, but trust me, and it's worth giving it a shot.

First things first, do your homework. Research the industry standards and salaries for your position. This will give you a solid understanding of what you should be aiming for. Knowledge is power, my friend!

Next, gather all the evidence to support your case. Highlight your accomplishments, any additional responsibilities you've taken on, and the value you bring to the company. Be prepared to articulate why you deserve a raise based on your performance and contributions.

Timing is crucial. Choose a strategic moment to have the conversation. Ideally, wait for a performance review or when you've recently achieved a significant milestone. This way, you can demonstrate your worth and show that you're invested in your growth within the company.

When you're ready to talk, approach your boss with confidence. Schedule a meeting to discuss your request. Be respectful and professional, but don't hesitate to express your desire for a raise. You can communicate your reasons and back them up with the evidence you've gathered.

Remember, negotiating is a two-way street. Be open to a discussion and be prepared to listen to your employer's perspective. They might have valid points or suggestions for alternative ways to increase your compensation, such as additional benefits or a bonus structure.

Lastly, be ready for any outcome. There's a chance that your request might not be met with an immediate "yes." If that happens, ask for feedback on how to increase your chances. Consider setting specific goals or milestones to work towards and establish a timeline for a follow-up discussion.

Negotiating a salary raise can be nerve-wracking, but it's an important step in advocating for yourself and your worth. Remember, you have nothing to lose and everything to gain. So go for it, and best of luck in securing that well-deserved raise

Earning extra income through side hustles

Earning extra income through side hustles has become increasingly popular in recent years. Whether you're looking to pay off debt, save for a vacation, or boost your financial stability, side hustles offer a flexible and accessible way to increase your earnings. This article will explore the concept of side hustles and their benefits and provide some popular examples to inspire you.

Side hustles are essentially part-time jobs or business ventures that individuals pursue alongside their primary source of income. The beauty of side hustles lies in their flexibility—they can be tailored to your interests, skills, and schedule. You can choose how much time and effort you want to invest, making it an ideal option for those with busy schedules or other commitments.

One of the significant benefits of side hustles is the potential for increased income. While the extra money can be used to cover immediate financial needs, it can also be channeled towards long-term goals, such as retirement savings or building an emergency fund. Side hustles provide an opportunity to diversify your income streams, reducing financial vulnerability and enhancing overall financial well-being.

Additionally, side hustles often involve pursuing a passion or interest, allowing you to explore your creativity and develop new skills. Whether it's freelance writing, graphic design, photography, or tutoring, side hustles enable you to turn your hobbies into a profitable venture. This not only provides a sense of fulfillment but also opens up possibilities for personal and professional growth.

Now, let's delve into some popular side hustle ideas:

- Freelancing: Offer your skills and services on platforms like Upwork, Fiverr, or Freelancer. This could include writing, graphic design, web development, social media management, or virtual assistance.

- Online tutoring: Share your expertise by providing online tutoring in subjects in which you excel. Numerous platforms connect tutors with students worldwide, such as VIPKid, Tutor.com, or Chegg.

- Airbnb hosting: If you have a spare room or property, consider renting it out on Airbnb. This can be an excellent way to generate extra income, particularly if you live in a popular tourist destination.

- Delivery services: Sign up as a driver for food delivery services like Uber Eats, DoorDash, or Grubhub. This allows you to earn money by delivering meals in your spare time.

- E-commerce: Set up an online store on platforms like Etsy or Shopify and sell handmade crafts, artwork, or unique products.

- Blogging or content creation: Start a blog or YouTube channel and monetize it through advertisements, sponsored content, or affiliate marketing. This requires consistent effort and time but can be rewarding in the long run.

- Pet sitting or dog walking: If you enjoy spending time with animals, offer your services as a pet sitter or dog walker. Many pet owners seek reliable individuals to care for their furry friends when they're away.

- Renting assets: If you own assets like cameras, musical instruments, or power tools you don't use frequently, consider renting them out to others through platforms like Fat Llama or ShareGrid.

Remember, building a successful side hustle requires dedication, discipline, and a willingness to adapt. It may take time to establish a steady income stream, but with perseverance and the right approach, your side hustle can flourish. Research and comply with any legal and tax obligations associated with your chosen side hustle.

Starting a Business

Starting a business is an exciting and potentially rewarding venture that allows individuals to pursue their entrepreneurial dreams, exercise creativity, and increase income. While it can be a challenging endeavor, with careful planning, determination, and the right approach, starting a business can be a fulfilling journey. Here are some of the key steps involved in starting a business.

- Idea Generation: The first step is to generate a business idea. Look for opportunities in the market, identify problems that need solutions, and consider your skills, expertise, and passions. Brainstorm ideas and evaluate their feasibility, market potential, and competitive landscape.

- Market Research: Once you have a business idea, conduct thorough market research. This involves studying your target market, understanding customer needs and preferences, analyzing competitors, and identifying unique selling points. Market research helps validate your business concept and shape your marketing and sales strategies.

- Business Plan: Develop a comprehensive business plan that outlines your goals, target audience, marketing strategies, operational details, and financial projections. A well-structured business plan is a roadmap and helps you communicate your vision to potential investors, partners, or lenders.

- Legal Structure: Choose a legal structure for your business, such as a sole proprietorship, partnership, limited liability company (LLC), or corporation. Research the legal requirements and regulations associated with your chosen structure and register your business accordingly.

- Financing: Determine the financial requirements of your business and explore funding options. These may include personal savings, loans from banks or financial institutions, angel investors, venture capital, or crowdfunding. Prepare a financial plan that includes startup costs, operating expenses, and revenue projections.

- Business Name and Branding: Select a memorable and relevant name for your business. Ensure the name is not already trademarked or in use by another company. Develop a strong brand identity, including a logo, tagline, and visual elements that reflect your business values and resonate with your target audience.

- Set Up Operations: Establish the necessary infrastructure for your business. This may include securing office or retail space, acquiring equipment and technology, setting up a website or e-commerce platform, and implementing efficient systems for day-to-day operations. Consider inventory management, supply chain, and customer relationship management.

- Marketing and Sales: Develop a marketing strategy to promote your business and attract customers. Determine the best channels to reach your target audience, such as digital marketing, social media, content marketing, email marketing, or traditional advertising. Create a sales strategy that outlines your pricing, distribution, and customer acquisition tactics.

- Hiring and Team Building: Assess your staffing needs and hire talented individuals who share your vision and complement your skill set. Build a strong team with the necessary expertise and ensure clear communication and alignment of goals. If starting alone, consider outsourcing tasks or collaborating with freelancers or contractors.

- Launch and Iterate: Launch your business with a soft opening or a grand opening event, depending on your industry. Collect feedback from early customers and use it to refine your products, services, and processes. Stay adaptable and be open to making necessary adjustments based on customer preferences and market dynamics.

- Continuous Learning and Growth: Embrace a mindset of continuous learning and improvement. Stay updated on industry trends, attend conferences or workshops, join relevant business communities, and seek advice from mentors or business coaches. Stay agile and evolve your business to stay competitive in the market.

Starting a business is a challenging but rewarding journey that requires passion, perseverance, and strategic planning. While risks are involved, with careful preparation and a customer-centric approach, you can increase your chances of success. Remember to stay focused, adaptable, and committed to your long-term vision while being open to seizing opportunities and navigating challenges along the way.

Chapter Six

Managing Your Credit

Credit plays a vital role in our financial lives. It affects our ability to secure loans, obtain favorable interest rates, and influence potential job opportunities. Properly managing your credit is essential for maintaining a healthy financial profile and achieving your financial goals.

Understanding your credit score and report

Your credit score and credit report are essential components of your financial life. They give lenders and creditors valuable information about your creditworthiness and financial history. Understanding how they work and what they can help you make informed decisions and take steps to improve your credit. Here's a breakdown of credit scores and reports:

Credit Score:

Your credit score is a numerical representation of your creditworthiness. It is typically calculated using a scoring model developed by Fair Isaac Corporation (FICO) or VantageScore. Credit scores generally range from 300 to 850, with higher scores indicating better creditworthiness. The factors that influence your credit score include:

1. Payment History: Your track record of making timely payments on credit accounts, such as loans and credit cards, significantly impacts your credit score. Late payments, defaults, or accounts in collections can lower your score.

2. Credit Utilization: This refers to the amount of available credit you're using. High credit card balances relative to your credit limits can negatively affect your score. It's recommended to keep your credit utilization ratio below 30%.

3. Length of Credit History: The length of time you've had credit accounts impacts your score. A longer credit history demonstrates your ability to manage credit over time. It's beneficial to maintain older credit accounts, as they contribute positively to your credit score.

4. Credit Mix: A diverse mix of credit accounts, such as credit cards, installment loans, and mortgages, can positively impact your credit score. Lenders want to see that you can handle different types of credit responsibly.

5. New Credit Inquiries: Whenever you apply for new credit, a hard inquiry is generated on your credit report. Multiple inquiries within a short period can temporarily lower your credit score. It's advisable to minimize unnecessary credit applications.

Credit Report:

Your credit report is a detailed record of your credit history. It contains information on your credit accounts, payment history, outstanding debts, and public records such as bankruptcies or tax liens. Key elements of your credit report include:

1. Personal Information: This includes your name, address, Social Security number, and date of birth. It's important to ensure this information is accurate, as errors could impact your credit.

2. Account Information: Your credit report lists all your credit accounts, such as credit cards, loans, and mortgages. It includes details like the creditor's name, account number, type of account, credit limit or loan amount, and payment history.

3. Payment History: Your credit report shows your payment history for each account, indicating whether payments were made on time or if there were any late or missed payments. Negative information, such as delinquencies, can stay on your report for up to seven years.

4. Public Records: If you've had any bankruptcies, tax liens, or court judgments, they will be reflected in your credit report. These public records can significantly impact your creditworthiness.

5. Inquiries: Your credit report lists hard inquiries (initiated by you when applying for credit) and soft inquiries (initiated by creditors for pre-approved offers). Soft inquiries don't impact your credit score, while hard inquiries may temporarily negatively affect you.

6. Dispute Information: If you've disputed any information on your credit report, the resolution of those disputes will be recorded. It's important to review this section to ensure errors have been corrected.

Regularly reviewing your credit report is crucial to identify any errors or signs of identity theft. You're entitled to a free annual credit report from each major credit bureau, which you can request at AnnualCreditReport.com.

Understanding your credit score and report empowers you to take control of your financial well-being.

Building and improving your credit

Building and improving your credit is an ongoing process that requires discipline and responsible financial management. Whether you're starting from scratch or looking to enhance your existing credit profile, here are some strategies to help you build and improve your credit:

1. Establish Credit: If you're new to credit or have a limited credit history, establish credit accounts. Consider applying for a secured credit card or a credit builder loan, where you make small monthly payments to build credit. Timely payments on these accounts will help you build a positive credit history.

2. Become an Authorized User: If someone you trust has a credit card with a long and positive payment history, you can

ask them to add you as an authorized user. This can help you benefit from their good credit behavior, as their account activity may be reported on your credit report as well.

3. Practice Responsible Credit Usage: Use credit accounts sparingly and responsibly. Keep your credit card balances low and aim to pay them off in full each month. Avoid maxing out your credit limits, as high credit utilization can negatively impact your credit score.

4. Pay Bills on Time: Consistently making timely payments is crucial for building and improving your credit. Late payments can severely damage your credit score and stay on your credit report for years. Set up reminders or automatic payments to ensure you never miss a due date.

5. Diversify Your Credit Mix: Having a mix of different types of credit, such as credit cards, installment loans, and mortgages, can demonstrate your ability to handle various financial responsibilities. However, only take on credit that you can manage responsibly and fits your financial situation.

6. Keep Old Accounts Open: Closing old credit accounts can shorten your credit history and impact your credit score. If you have older accounts with positive payment history, consider keeping them open. They contribute to the length of your credit history and showcase your creditworthiness.

7. Monitor Your Credit Regularly: Stay vigilant by monitoring your credit reports and scores regularly. Check for errors, inaccuracies, or signs of identity theft. Many websites and financial institutions offer free credit score monitoring services, or you can obtain your free credit reports annually from the major credit bureaus.

8. Limit New Credit Applications: Applying for multiple credit accounts quickly can raise concerns for lenders and negatively impact your credit score. Only apply for credit when necessary and when you are confident of meeting the obligations.

9. Use Credit-Building Tools: Some financial institutions and credit card companies offer credit-building tools or programs to help individuals establish or rebuild credit. Explore these options to accelerate your credit-building efforts.

10. Be Patient and Persistent: Building and improving credit takes time. It's important to be patient and persistent in your efforts. Consistently practicing good credit habits and making responsible financial choices will gradually improve your creditworthiness.

Using credit responsibly

While building and improving your credit, it's crucial to understand the importance of using credit responsibly. Responsible credit usage not only helps maintain a good credit score but also sets the foundation for long-term financial stability. Here are some key principles to follow when using credit:

1. Borrow Only What You Can Afford: Before taking on any credit, carefully evaluate your financial situation. Consider your income, expenses, and existing debts. Borrow only what you can comfortably repay within the specified terms. Avoid the temptation to max out your credit cards or take on excessive debt.
2. Create and Stick to a Budget: Developing a budget allows you to track your income and expenses, ensuring you have enough funds to cover your credit

obligations. It helps you prioritize your spending, avoid overspending, and stay on top of your financial goals. Adjust your budget as needed to accommodate your credit payments.

3. Pay in Full and on Time: Pay your credit card balances monthly to avoid unnecessary interest charges. If paying in full is not feasible, make at least the minimum payment on time to maintain a positive payment history. Late or missed payments can significantly negatively impact your credit score.

4. Minimize Credit Utilization: Keeping your credit utilization ratio low is crucial. Aim to use only a small portion of your available credit. High credit utilization can signal financial distress and lower your credit score. Regularly review your credit card balances and make payments to keep them as low as possible.

5. Avoid Opening Unnecessary Credit Accounts: While having a mix of credit types is beneficial, opening multiple new credit accounts within a short period can raise concerns for lenders. Each new application results in a hard inquiry, temporarily lowering your credit score. Only open new accounts when

necessary and consider the potential impact on your credit.

6. Be Cautious with Co-Signing: Co-signing a loan or credit card for someone else makes you equally responsible for the debt. Before co-signing, understand the potential risks and implications. If the primary borrower defaults or makes late payments, it can negatively impact your credit and financial well-being.

7. Regularly Review Your Statements and Reports: Stay vigilant by reviewing your credit card and loan statements regularly. Look for any discrepancies or unauthorized charges that may indicate fraud. Additionally, monitor your credit reports for accuracy and address any errors promptly.

8. Use Credit-Building Tools Wisely: Credit-building tools, such as secured credit cards or credit builder loans, can help establish building credit. However, use them responsibly. Make timely payments and keep balances low to maximize their positive impact on your credit history.

9. Avoid Excessive Credit Inquiries: Applying for new credit generates hard

inquiries on your credit report. While one or two inquiries are generally manageable, a large number within a short period can raise red flags for lenders. Limit your credit applications to those necessary and align with your financial goals.

Maintain a Long-Term Perspective: Building and maintaining good credit is a continuous process. Practice responsible credit usage consistently over time, and it will help you establish a strong credit history. This will enable you to access better credit terms and opportunities in the future.

Chapter Seven

Review of Key Points

Assessing Your Current Financial Situation
The first chapter of "Mastering Your Finances" focuses on understanding and assessing one's financial situation. The author emphasizes the importance of recognizing income and expenses accurately, analyzing debt and savings, and identifying areas for improvement. By providing practical tools and exercises, readers are encouraged to gain a clear understanding of their financial standing, laying a solid foundation for the subsequent chapters.

In Chapter 2, the book delves into creating a budget. The author highlights the significance of setting financial goals and guides readers through developing a monthly budget. Furthermore, the book emphasizes the importance of tracking expenses and adjusting the budget. By offering practical tips and strategies, readers have the knowledge and tools to manage their finances effectively.

Debt reduction is a common financial challenge many individuals face, and Chapter 3 addresses this issue comprehensively. The book provides readers with various strategies for paying off debt, such as snowballs and avalanches.

Additionally, it explores debt consolidation options and advises avoiding future debt. By offering a variety of approaches, readers can choose the methods that best suit their circumstances.

Building savings is a crucial aspect of achieving financial stability, and Chapter 4 delves into this topic. The author stresses the importance of setting up an emergency fund and saving for long-term goals. Moreover, the book provides insights into investment options for the future. By outlining practical steps and offering valuable advice, readers are encouraged to take proactive measures to secure their financial future.

Chapter 5 addresses the issue of increasing income, which can greatly contribute to financial stability. The book explores various methods, such as negotiating a salary raise, pursuing side hustles, and even starting a business. By presenting diverse options, the author empowers readers to identify opportunities for income growth, ultimately enhancing their financial well-being.

Effective credit management is a vital aspect of financial stability, and Chapter 6 provides readers with the necessary knowledge and tools to navigate this area successfully. The book explains the significance of understanding credit scores and reports guides readers on building and improving their credit, and emphasizes responsible credit usage. By demystifying the complexities of credit management, readers are empowered to make informed decisions and avoid common pitfalls.

Encouragement to continue working toward financial stability

It's important to remember that achieving financial stability is a journey that requires patience, dedication, and perseverance. While the road may have challenges, every step you take toward improving your financial situation brings you closer to a more secure and prosperous future.

By actively implementing the strategies outlined in "Mastering Your Finances: A Comprehensive Guide to Financial Stability," you are already committed to your financial well-being. Take pride in your efforts and use them as fuel to keep moving forward. Remember that small changes and consistent actions can yield significant results over time.

During this journey, it's essential to stay focused on your goals and maintain a positive mindset. There may be obstacles and setbacks, but don't let them discourage you. Instead, view them as opportunities for growth and learning. Remember that financial stability is achievable, and every challenge you overcome brings you one step closer to your desired outcome.

Celebrate your achievements, no matter how small they may seem. Whether it's paying off debt, successfully sticking to a budget, or increasing your savings, acknowledge and reward yourself for your progress. This positive reinforcement will help to motivate and encourage you to continue on your path toward financial stability.

Surround yourself with a support system of like-minded individuals who share similar financial goals. Engage in discussions, seek advice, and learn from others who have successfully navigated their financial journeys. By connecting with others on a similar path, you'll find inspiration, accountability, and valuable insights to enhance your progress further.

Lastly, remember that financial stability is not just about accumulating wealth but also about achieving peace of mind and freedom. It's about having the resources and confidence to pursue your dreams, provide for your loved ones, and live a fulfilling life. Keep your vision of financial stability in mind, and let it constantly remind you of the brighter future that awaits you.

So, continue to stay committed, stay focused, and stay determined. Your efforts for outward financial stability are worthwhile, and with each step you take, you create a more secure and prosperous future for yourself. Believe in your ability to succeed, and never underestimate the power of your actions and decisions. Keep going, and you'll find that the rewards of financial stability are well worth the journey.

Conclusion

In conclusion, "Mastering Your Finances: A Comprehensive Guide to Financial Stability" is a valuable resource that equips readers with the knowledge and tools to navigate the path toward financial stability. By addressing common financial challenges and providing practical strategies, the book empowers individuals to take control of their finances and work towards a more secure and prosperous future.

Remember, achieving financial stability is a process that requires time, effort, and commitment. Embrace the journey and stay motivated, even in the face of challenges. Celebrate your achievements along the way, and don't hesitate to seek support from others who share similar goals.

By implementing the strategies outlined in the book and staying dedicated to your financial well-being, you are taking important steps toward creating a better future for yourself and your loved ones. Financial stability is not just about accumulating wealth; it's about gaining peace of mind, having the freedom to pursue your dreams, and living a fulfilling life.

So, continue to educate yourself, make informed decisions, and adapt your strategies as needed. With each action you take, you are building a stronger foundation for your financial stability. Believe in yourself, stay focused, and never lose sight of the brighter future.

Remember, financial stability is within your reach, and "Mastering Your Finances" provides the guidance and support you need to make it a reality. Start your journey today and enjoy the rewards of achieving financial stability.

About Author

Zakari, an accomplished entrepreneur in the food processing industry, has embarked on a mission to educate individuals about the challenges of starting a business and the intricacies of managing finances. With a burning passion for empowering others with knowledge, he has ventured into the realm of professional writing, using his expertise to create educative business and guidebooks for a diverse range of clients.

Having successfully established his own food processing industry, Zakari brings invaluable firsthand experience to his writing. He understands the numerous obstacles that entrepreneurs encounter on their journey, from navigating the complexities of business operations to effectively managing financial resources. Armed with this knowledge, he aims to impart valuable insights to aspiring entrepreneurs and business owners, equipping them with the necessary tools to overcome hurdles and achieve their goals.

Zakari's entrepreneurial spirit extends beyond his own ventures. Recognizing the power of education and its potential to transform lives, he is driven by a desire to reach a broad audience with his message. By joining freelance networks as a writer, he has embraced a platform that enables him to share his expertise on a global scale. Through his writing, he strives to educate and inspire individuals from all walks of life, irrespective of their background or circumstances.

The core belief that underpins Zakari's work is his unwavering faith in the potential for success that lies within every individual. He firmly believes that with the right guidance and steps, anyone can accomplish their dreams and aspirations in business or any endeavor they pursue. This guiding principle fuels his writing, as he seeks to provide actionable advice and practical strategies that can be applied by his readers to enhance their business acumen and financial literacy.

Zakari's writing not only reflects his profound understanding of entrepreneurship and finance but also embodies his dedication to empowering others. He recognizes the transformative power of education and aims to make a lasting impact by equipping individuals with the knowledge and skills necessary to navigate the complex world of business.

In his journey as an author, entrepreneur, and educator, Zakari's commitment to excellence shines through. Through his writings, he seeks to empower and uplift, illuminating the path to success for aspiring entrepreneurs and individuals seeking to improve their financial acumen. With his invaluable insights and genuine passion for education, Zakari is poised to make a significant impact in the world of business and finance, guiding others towards their own achievements and fulfilling their entrepreneurial ambitions.

www.ingramcontent.com/pod-product-compliance
Lightning Source LLC
Chambersburg PA
CBHW031542210526
45464CB00003B/1116